Healing Heart

Poems 1973-1988
by Gloria T. Hull

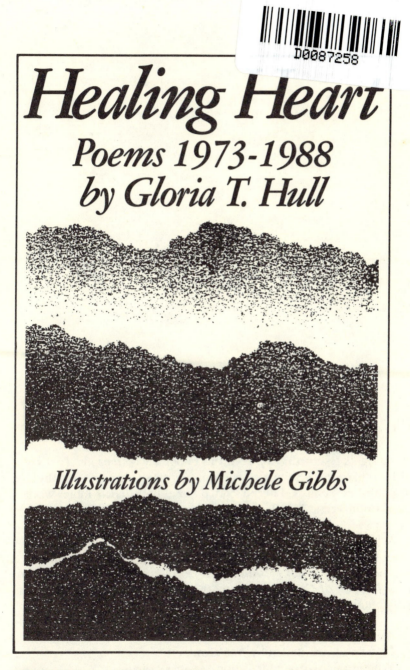

Illustrations by Michele Gibbs

KITCHEN TABLE: Women of Color Press

Acknowledgement is given to the following journals in which some of these poems first appeared: *Callaloo, Conditions, Frontiers: A Journal of Women's Studies, Hoo-Doo, Ikon, Obsidian, Pathways: A Journal of Creative Writing* (Kingston, Jamaica), *Sol/Inner Sol, Women: A Journal of Liberation.*

Illustrations by Michele Gibbs.
Cover and text design by Ann Cammett.
Typesetting by Communication Services, Albany, N.Y.

First Edition. First Printing.

ISBN 0-913175-16-1

Healing Heart

Poems 1973-1988 by Gloria T. Hull

Also by Gloria T. Hull

All the Women Are White, All the Blacks Are Men, But Some of Us Are Brave: Black Women's Studies, Co-editor with Patricia Bell Scott and Barbara Smith (The Feminist Press).

Give Us Each Day: The Diary of Alice Dunbar-Nelson, Editor.

Color, Sex, and Poetry: Three Women Writers of the Harlem Renaissance.

The Works of Alice Dunbar-Nelson, Editor.

Table of Contents

Family Pictures

Roots—#1 1
The Taste of Mother Love 2
Pictures My Mother Left Me, Growing Up 4
Triptych 11
Blues Snatch 13
The Dishes 14
For Nothing 16
Movin' and Steppin' 18
Neighbor Lady 20
Acknowledgement: Three Graces 21
Thinking—In Part—About Toni Morrison 24
Poem for Audre 25
Her/Story 27
Witches and Queers 29
The Prison and the Park 30

Friends—and Other Lovers

It's too bad 37
What My Honey Says 38
Miss Houdini 39
Brother Man 40
Ron 42
The Cusp of Feeling 44
From Running Come Touch 45
For Konda in Jamaica 46
Who Is This Dude 47
Saint Chant 49
we love in circles 50

The Carroll Poems

A Poem About Hooking Up 55
Waking With the Princess 56
I Want You 58
Muse 60
Loving (In Place) 62
Fasting 64
Totem and tattoo 66

Jamaica Journal

The Bear	71
Love Words: Spoken	72
At My Age	74
Zora in Accompong	76
Bluestime: Allusions	77
Dear Pastor	78
Short Poem	81
Sister to pain, and not unacquainted with grief	82
Soothing An Unquiet Spirit	84
"And life...": A Story	86
A Jazz Poem	88
Ongiving	91
When Storm Clouds Gather	93
Welcome Home	95
Of peace, I say	97

Healing Heart

Invocation	103
Young Girls' Blues	104
The Rice and Peas Farewell	113
The Way It Is (Right Now)	115
Counting Cost	116
Ron II	120
Somebody, Some Body	121
Being Clear About It	122
Another Rhythm	123
You, Too	124
Who told you...?	125
Pants For True	126
About Grandmothers and Mothers	127
Legacy/Repeat After Me	129
Good Question	132
Dumping Harry Claggett	134
Crossing	137
When Trees Talk	138
Meeting the Self	139
8-5-88	140

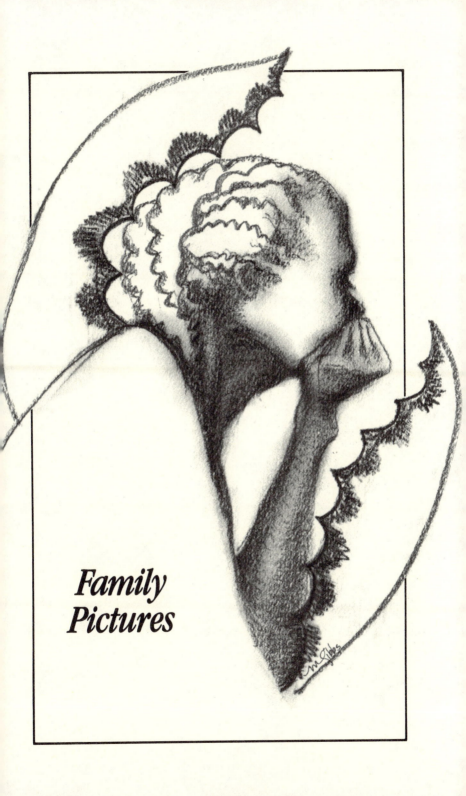

*Family
Pictures*

Roots—#1

Asthmatic Madam Blue
with her crooked oil can

She could minister to your scalp
and grow hair
on arid temples

Had a "shop"
across the Looney Street ditch
and made her close back room
a trysting place for mother
in her salad days

There my father seeded me
his last Louisiana spring

The Taste of Mother Love

i.   Dialogue: A Question and an Answer

Q. How come my food don't taste like yours?
A. That's the mother love in it, honey.

ii.   The Fact

Make no mistake about it:
Mother love has taste.

That's what
> seasons the beans
> and salts the roast
> and makes the cabbage taste good
> (even when they're just cooked in bacon grease).

It's what
> you yearn for on separated holidays
> rush back to on vacations
> and what makes you fat
> (when you stay there too long).

It's why
> you beg for a bite off mama's plate
> (right after you finish cleaning your own)
> and why home for you will always be
> your mother's yellow, broken-backed kitchen.

iii. Learning Experience

I sit in my mama's kitchen, watching her cook.

Did you brown the meat before you set it in the oven?
How much onion did you put in that dressing?

Do you use milk or water in your cornbread? any eggs?
And how many spoons of sugar did it take to make the potatoes
    this sweet?

What made your stew go from thin to thick like that?
Sometimes mine never does, no matter how long and slow I cook
    it.

My mother is a patient woman;
she cooks and answers,
sometimes even in measurements and minutes—
if I keep pinning her down.

Later, I stand in my own kitchen, trying to cook.
I do it just so, remembering and following exactly everything
    mama said.

BUT THEN, MY FOOD JUST WON'T TASTE LIKE HERS.

That's why when anybody says
cooking is a science,
I know better.

Ever been served contentment in a laboratory?
And any fool can tell you:
Real mother love don't grow on trees.

▼

Pictures My Mother
Left Me,
Growing Up

i.

Momma
as a young girl
listening—fast gal—
to what the big women said:
about husbands who beat them
men who were mean
run-around lovers
and other such female burdens

Later, to her granny,
saying
"Mama, Mama,
you know what I'd do
if I had a husband like that?
I'd wait 'til he was sleep at night
and pour hot lye down his ear."

"Shut up, gal,
Ain't no man gon want to marry
nobody crazy as you!"

March, 1944
Saturn's been vexing Pisces
ordering old deaths
and a fresh new star

This thirtieth birthday
sweet tart, hot young thing
flown the East Texas coop
for city life in Louisiana

The slick paramour, the nighttime gambler
afternoon meeting in a good friend's steamy back room
(she wanted, she said, to see her man before he left)

Belly baby full,
she still refused to follow him—
She needed the love
but didn't quite feel like going
to California

iii.

Of her
as a new wife—
husband twenty years older
lying sick in a hospital bed

Every day she caught the incommodious bus.

One morning
she got up looking at their Packard
standing idle as a horse
in the brightening yard:

"It don't make sense
for me to have that car
just setting out there like that.
I'm going to get in it
and drive."

Gears scraped the first days' practice—
but she's been driving ever since

One of Alice Walker's "headragged generals"
storming the schoolyard gates
Soapsuds from the washtub
dry-ringing her sleeveless arms,
the front of her old print housedress
still wet with sweat and pungent blue rinsing water

The cafeteria manager
hadn't fed my brother lunch
that day,
something about rules and eligibility—
nothing which sounded right
next to her baby's empty stomach

The manager's double derriere quivered
the big pots and pans rattled
on the cafeteria walls:
"If I ever hear
that you let my child go hungry,
I will wring your neck
and tear this whole place down!"

Then
there was the time when she jumped out of the car
breaking up a fight
between me and Carolyn,
a lanky gal who towered over me
and didn't like my high-90's air

The principal caught mother knuckling Carolyn,
intruded his slim dark body and frantic words:
"Miz Thompson, Miz Thompson," he cried
"Don't you know they can put you in jail?"

"Jail, jail, who's afraid of jails?"
she shouted
"They was made for people, wu'nt they?
They wu'nt made for cats and dogs!"

Many years later, the two of them laughed together:
Little 'Fessor Green said,
"I sure was glad
when all of your children
left my school."

                              v.

Her final solution was always the same:

To whatever demeaning thing it was
which threatened her dignity and self—
            white people's slavery
            black male suppression
            starvation wages for soul-killing work
she had one stock defiance:

"Before I do that
I'll eat sh--
with a splinter."

Buying warmth for sprouting children,
she didn't always have for herself
a real decent winter coat

But what she loved were hats:

Fifty-dollar "Mr. John's"
razored wickedly over one dark eye,
hand-me-down knit caps
pulled colorfully across
however she wore her heavy hair

"Anything I throw on my head,"
she said
"looks good on me."

vii.

Letters like this:

"We just stopped talking, my dear
I cut that President mess off (ha ha)

Well, honey
I hate to hear you talking
about how tired you are
Everybody's tired these days
that's working
So much stress and strain

We can't give up,
it will ease up
one day

I have really been to the place
I've felt like giving up,
just couldn't go another further,
but I've stood in the floor
with both hands up
and said
as the hymn we sing in church—
Father I stretch my hands to thee
          No other help I know—
And I'm still hanging on

I love you so much

Be sweet,

          Mother Dear"

▼

Triptych

My baby, my boy
my dusty-black darling—
I don't write
many poems about you

The words hide thinly
inside my heart
and mutely succumb to your legs'
stubborn beauty

Your babyhood is a blur
of sunshine on a hill

Then, I knew you daily

Now I blink through the distance
to see you—
grown tall enough to crown
your father's love

ii.

Seventeen years later
I'm still bleeding on your birthday

My mother could have told me
My mother probably did tell me
(but in her coded way)
that having children is one constant flow
           of rusty blood

When this dark stuff stops coming
look for the telltale spots—
the mute stigmata—
in my heart

iii.

This shining young man
(the astrologer said)
used to be my father
is now my son
whom I could wish
for husband
so fine,
so fine

v

Blues Snatch

I woke up this morning
With a bad taste in my mind
'Woke up this morning
Bad taste in my mind
If tears would wash it away, honey
Maybe I'd get to crying.

I got some real big troubles
So I sing these imitation blues
I got trouble, trouble, trouble
That's why I sing the blues.
If I could play me a guitar
I'd go and spread the news.

I'd say "Lord have mercy
Lord have mercy on me."
B.B. cried, "Lord have mercy
Lord have mercy on me."
Why don't you send down some good times
And tell these blues to let me be.

I'd been fighting off misery on the left side
Until I could hardly stand
Looked around and there was the blues
Coming to shake my other hand.

I got trouble, trouble, trouble
That's why I sing the blues
I got real bad trouble
So I sing the blues
With the luck I been having lately
Won't matter if I win or lose.

▼

The Dishes

It's going to be the dishes—
quietly fouling the kitchen air

the ones
you leave half-dirty
and ticking
on the counter top

innocuous plates and boilers
a haphazard pile of evidence
as damaging as the exhibit
at a first-degree murder trial

the baked-on skillet grease
spreading
like mildew or anger

rust fit to match
the rings and spots
slowly dotting the earthenware crocks

near cousins
to the easier, sleazier
egg yolk, scorched rice, honey print
the other dubious stains
which smile and conceal nothing

All these pieces of contention
which we hurl each time
with a more practiced
and deadly aim
scoring
excoriating
the wide fields
of our difference

They make walking
in the living and dining rooms dangerous—
Sleeping upstairs, we take
freshly corroded breaths

It's not the symbol itself
but what it means
that carries the freight

It's going to be the dishes
finally
that break
this camel's back

For Nothing

When nothing
is better than something

When nothing becomes
the something sought

The silence
one doesn't have
to ask for

The chair warm
with just one body's heat

Time uncontoured, unshared
Unspent spaces coaxing
the waiting lines

Only one's own yawn—
One fork falling

A single set of muddy footprints,
solitary rain drops on the floor—
No angles trespassing
on the peaceful bed

No handy object
for generalized anger,
and freedom to trace the madness
to its primal source

Relief from the weight
of someone waiting—
for the bathtub,
attention,
the room
one wants to call
one's own

Movin' and Steppin'

There are times when
one needs to move—
to newer places
wider spaces

exchange the pond
        for the ocean
and jump right in
(it don't matter if your hair
gets wet or briny)

Mothers can tell you
shoes get too tight
and clothes grow old

How can you be Cinderella
        in the same tired frumpy frog gown
let alone Nerfertiti or Cleopatra
        conquering the Nile

It just won't do.

Generally speaking,
it's hard for people's eyes
        to readjust
There you stand—
        a brand new *thang*
and they keep talking to someone
        you left behind long time ago
        (and swear you never want to see again)

Jive action like that
can push you back—
into the Dark Ages, a closet,
some fancy trickbag or claustrophobic hole

Take a stroll
down different streets
where there are flowers that you can't name
and sights you've never seen before

Where the air breathes fresher
        and people take you for a stranger

And you can keep on walking
hightime stepping getting up walking
into that future self
you got to be

Neighbor Lady

Flowered diagonals and tartan plaids
war fiercely and most alarmingly
in her dress

Unconscious of the battle,
she occupies her own peculiar field,
keeping house against the two grown sons and husband
who threaten to overrun

Acknowledgement: Three Graces *

i.

Georgia In My Dreams

The dark bottom of the slumbering ocean
is a mirror
Sea mirror, densely shining
Come—and see
Georgia Douglas Johnson
sorceress treading through my sleeping
treading lightly
calling
dreaming me

She walked me through her narrow hallway
dusty with papers
as easy in the piles of clutter
as a witch's cat

She wanted me to know that
though they burned them for her funeral
she woman wrote every poem, play, novel, story
that we were stepping over

Wanted me to know—before I saw it—
that her Half-way House still held her
that the red-pink roses she had planted
should not die

---

* Written for Georgia Douglas Johnson, Angelina Weld Grimké, and
Alice Dunbar-Nelson, three poets-writers of the Harlem Renaissance.

21

If Two

for Angelina

If I could paint this in words
I'd be like Angelina
These were the scenes she loved
This gorgeous sunset parading itself
      across the evening sky
Lighting up orange flares and cobalt streamers
Thin-needled pine stalks
      gently fingering the blue
Lining layers of subtle color
      even prettier than a rainbow
Saffron, bright amber, pure amethyst, beryl hues

Angelina, you favored these delicate shades
Seeking clear chromatics for the dissonant half-tones
      of your strangely muted life

The tints are vibrant still
      behind this darkening curtain
The gracile pines—their mood now changed to indigo—
      are menacing the night

Miss Alice

She loves me, she loves me not
She loves me, she loves me not

Stuck up 'risto lady
with your snub-turned nose and your fancy clothes
I wouldn't speak to you either
if I passed you on the street
My hair's too wild,
my skin is dark
So why did you bother me?
And why did I bother you?—
Clanging in your boxes and your unquiet bed

Those press releases were not enough
You wanted the whole damn story, the record set straight
Your daring rescued from the backyards and the barbeques
You knew your stellar spot was center stage

But I still don't really like you, queenly lady
(Lady, how do you feel about me?)
Yet if I said we were not sisters
Rain curses, Goddess strike me
for telling one awful lie

Thinking—In Part—About Toni Morrison

There is your power name
Your praise name
Your peace name

Your real name
Your love name

The name your mama gave you
The name they wrote down
        on the birth certificate

The nickname your uncles call you
The nickname your sister calls you
Your name on the block
And your most secret name
        (whispered only to yourself)

Long before Freud discovered multiple identities
We understood the many aspects of the soul

And we didn't ever call nobody
out of their
right name

▼

Poem for Audre

What you said keeps bothering me
keeps needling, grinding
like toothache
or a bad
conscience:

> "Your silence
> will not
> protect you"

> "Our speaking is stopped
> because we fear the visibility
> without which
> we can not really live"

You quietly stand there,
annealed by death,
mortality shining:

> "Whether we speak or not,
> the machine will crush us to bits—
> and we will also
> be afraid"

> "Your silence
> will not
> protect you"

Some of us—
we dumb autistic ones,
the aphasics,
those who can only stutter
or point,
some who speak in tongues,
or write in invisible ink—
sit rigid, our eyelids burning—
mute
from birth
from fear
from habit
for love and money
for children
for fear
for fear

while you probe
our agonized silence,
a constant pain:

>Dear Eshu's Audre,
>please keep on teaching us
>how
>to speak,
>to know
>that now
>"our labor *is*
>more important than
>our silence."

V

Her/Story

She told me her story
the same old story
of the telephone number
and the innocent, empty house
the ordinary kitchen
the plain table turned operating room

How the thing hurt
the hanger and the packing
trying to brave wait the days
until it all came out
in the dormitory toilet
roommates laughing
on either side of the stall

I'm thinking about Dean Harris
all the other barely legal
deans of women
watching the parade of black girls
coeds passing with three and four month swellings
saying nothing—much—because time will tell

The lucky ones got through
made it to the next step, the next year
the ones like her
telling me this story
I didn't truly want to hear
too close to the secrets
of my own violated womb

"In there with the blood and gauze
was this baby, this real teeny baby"
she said
"and I flushed it all down"

Why didn't the toilets stop up
with all those babies?
Progress Hall stink in a flood
of blood and pain?—
blind eyes and tied tongues
shrieked wide open
by the shredded bodies
floating from under the beds

Like the scandal
whispering through my girlhood
of all the bone babies
they found in the walls
when they tore down the nuns' house
at my Catholic elementary school

▼

Witches and Queers

Gotta go
Get burned at night
Get thrown in rivers
      ditches, oceans
down wells and airshafts
      old abandoned mines

Abandoned to police night sticks
      loose boys on the block
      neighborhood ladies' clean up leagues
      judges, juries, panels of their peers
      and other illegal and legal inquisitions

Witches and queers

Make waves
Learn how to swim
      how to walk on water
      fight back

Know the codes
Read the signs
Signal salvation with
      a blood-red handkerchief flying
      against blue jeans and the velvet dark
        of the moon

▼

The Prison and the Park*

The park
The broiling Miami park
Grass—
What's underfoot
and curling up in smoke
between Black lips

One frustrated square of people
asking
"Where is justice?"
(for the dead Black beaten businessman:
four white cops)
"Where are our leaders?"

Where is the love?

Certainly not lurking
outside the smoldering "war zone"

The violence is contained.

White Miami retreats
        into an armed camp
The Black community surrounded
        by 4,000 M-16's—
No drugstores, food stores, buses,
        liquor stores, gas stations,
        Burger Kings or Dairy Queens

---

*Information and quotes taken from two news stories in the
 Washington *Post,* Tuesday, May 20, 1980.

The tactic is clear
        and ancient:
occupation, isolation, neutralization

Crosstown the leaders huddle:
The brothers and sisters at the park
        are doing their thing. "I don't know
        what that is,"
the head leader says.

"They want to find out
        what we're doing."
The women always know—
        and speak the truth

Meanwhile
Governor Mandel enters Eglin federal prison
"with a wave over his shoulder
and a tight-lipped smile"

He will stay in the Florida panhandle
maybe four or five months

Long enough to mow the lawn,
get a good suntan,
smoke his pipes

Then, writes the Washington *Post,*
"after he learns how to make his bed
and master prison regulations,
Mandel will graduate
to one of four new carpeted
and air-conditioned dormitories
that offer privacy cubicles
where each inmate has a bunk
and a built-in...bookcase."

He can make unlimited phone calls
            (collect)
write uncensored letters
            (as long as he buys his own stamps)
purchase tobacco, slippers, sunglasses,
coffee mugs, shaving equipment, iced tea,
cookies, pickles and peanuts.

But, according to officials,
Eglin is not an "exclusive haven
for white collar prisoners."

At least 12% Black
            get in.

The officials didn't say
if Blacks also bought up
the commissary tennis balls—
cheap.

▼

*Friends—
and
Other
Lovers*

It's too bad

It's too bad, I think
(usually in a space filled with others)
that my life
looks like this
People are going to think
that my life is
what it looks like

What-my-life-looks-like
says
"I don't think you need to worry about
what people think"

Philosophers call this
appearance versus reality

Most times I say it's just
a crying shame

What My Honey Says

My honey says I'm sweet
And my honey calls me pretty
And my honey even tells me
"Girl, you take me out!"

My honey squeezes me up
          and likes me little
rubs my curves
          and calls them fine.
And my honey loves me good
          just because I'm so nice
          to do it to.

In bed my honey looks hard at me
And kisses me so soft I feel like crying
Then turns around and tells me
I'm one hell of a piece.

But...still...
I don't really think I'm cute
And I don't like to ego trip.
It's just that sometimes
I tend to believe
What my honey says.

Miss Houdini

Now you see her
and now you don't

My Houdini
of the Heart-Space

Disappearing
at her own
sweet will

Leaving holes
       all   over
the   place

I just got tired
of being surprised
with nothing

Hey, Miss Houdini

I'm checking out
the act
next door

Brother Man

for E'bert

He writes the kind of poetry
a man would write
if he were a woman

The first time I heard it
it freaked me out

I'm still astonished—
reading about Joseph
whose child will be taken away

And thinking on those other men
who cry each month
and wonder if their protective shields
are still in place

No,
wanting to take them off
for love birthing trust
in the slow-dripping tallow
between a good wife's thighs

Some men could be women—
but I guess that wouldn't be fair—
to the other side

For women loving men
need women, too

Easy-breaking smiles, soft voices,
laughing details which hold life to the ground—
a spirit which connects
and stands up to the seasons

Like the brother who writes these poems
who makes me think maybe
some men can be sisters

V

Ron

He had a Jesus face
with a beard which would have been red
and mild, two-colored eyes
(which also laughed
got scared and suffered)

I don't know if he had
the gift of healing,
but he laid his hand
like a prayer
on my swollen belly
and raised an amen
in my startled breast

He had a hairless body,
was a furniture-moving, basketball-playing Adonis,
was sleek and hard and
gleamed like olive oil—
and each time I lay with him
I thought
"No, saints can't love
like sinners can"—
but gave him my purest blessing anyway

He talked with a hoosier boy's accent
which you couldn't hear in his poetry
although you could see it sometime
when he faced the world

He reverenced all people and all places
in his life
(as Feliciano sang them to him)
and delighted in Dylan's ladies
and his big brass bed—
"And if all my dreams come true,
I'll be spending time with you"

He loved stories (couldn't tell them)
and children (made two)
and thought his dark-haired wife
was the givingest woman born

While I kept the faith
he went through changes
and finally became this sadness
in my throat

V

The Cusp of Feeling

"You're the find of my life;
I know it sounds corny
but I love you"—

—through the room of boxes
and the half-ajar door
which shuts off cats and yearnings
listing smoothly on the cool night air
making solid the reasons why
      there is this wall
through the common space of kitchen
where we say goodnight
and speak next morning in the definite tones of light
(note: in this poem—as in real life—
your bedroom is a mine field,
uneasy ground left better unexplored)

you lie there
unconscious (conscious?) of this moorless thread
unwinding in my chest—
later take your place beside me
in a sleeping bag upon the floor:
one hazy moment of clear communication,
a touch as fugitive as the hug we use
to greet and say goodbye:
"I'm writing a poem," I answer—
talking to you like always
in the silences of things
      I want to say—
to say that I have room here for you
in the cusp of feeling
rising between my breasts

▼

From Running Come Touch

for M.

You told me about
your fear of penetration—
men's maleness, people pushing
all thrusts you warded off
with weapons
your mother handed you
through pain

But, then, you touched me—
amazing move—
your shy sure fingers
unbalancing my reasons,
teeth biting off my breath

It was darkness come
daylight come morning
instinct and body love
coming through hands
and breakfast and
questions leading nowhere
more clothes and passion
cocaine frost
the cat licking salmon
back darkness back rubbing
lessons hanging out pleasure
from running coming touching
deep
      into

▼

For Konda in Jamaica

If I wanted you
a weight of brass and copper
on my arm
or three days wearing soreness
in my ear
I could have it—
Or take the pain
of too much loving
not enough
from my unruly wants
your wanting madness

Always against—always—
a music of
jazz and disco tunes incessant
crazy people
tipsy plans
and scatter—
And always you, girlfriend
your round-eyed slant of beauty
smoothing
searching out the certainty
        in my face
with riddled answers burning
        through your own—

Woman—precious, special woman

What happens in Jamaica
        when the sun goes down?
When will I see you again
        oh, sweet delight of my eyes?

▼

Who Is This Dude

Who is this dude?
Who is this Black dude?
          Nikki Giovanni

He could be
jive around the edges
just another scared colored man
who doesn't know what to do
with an awesome sister who loves him
and won't tell lies

Maybe that way of talking like an oracle
sitting like a new guru
is a yoga pose masking a knee-deep shuffle
New Age turning backwards into old slave games

Could that downplaying of the bed
the sublimation of the sexual self
into higher realms
be just another light way out?—
the exit of the little white men who invented celibacy
to curtail the power of women

Maybe this fine fresh image
I'm calling my brother/my lover/my self
is the familiar figure
who darkened my mother's doorstep many nights ago
and clouded my sister's dreams of happiness
for a do-right man

I could be wrong about all this
but I think I'll think about it
this fugitive writing her own slick narrative
on the way to freedom

Saint Chant

Against your black shoulder
body quirky as a woman's

Muffled, still
picking responsibility from apple vines
heavy as stones
I take the weight

You can't bear it
can't bear me
opening like dark-thighed marble
pouring rivers oceans seas
sucking you in
and under—

primeval nightmares
men have always had:
the disappearance of the bone
annihilation of the self
in a swirl of blood
flooding

Look
I can't help this love
can't harness my passion

Flow with me—
or hold us drowning under—
chanting like the saint you are

we love in circles

we love in circles
        touching round—

faces in a ritual ring
        echoing blood and color
nappy girlheads in a summer porch swing
belligerent decisions to live
        and be ourselves

first within, then out of
the bands which grow too tight—
gold multiplying lovers
        costing us dear

serious commitments to own, to other
to chaos and the maelstrom
winding deep
swirling sunspots blinding
like the first real kiss
in a room of strangers

voices a refrain:
        Their marriage has lasted five years now
        (the community helps keep them together)

        I'm committed to non-monogamy, one woman said
        Then she (non-monogamy, not the woman)
            became the new girl on the block

        A comes before B—now you remember that
            Mother Kettle says—
        But also C D E F G J K and Y,
        I caught up in the middle
            courting doom

we become one crazy geographic crazy quilt:
Washington, D. C. and New York City
a two-sided circle
return trips rounding it out
roping in Philly and Boston,
Cleveland and the Coast
ringing the world—
a daisy chain
       of legs and mattress edges
                looping

we love in circles
passing it on—
palm up turned down, palm up turned down,
       palm up turned down, palm up turned down...
passing it on—
       all the strength
       the knowledge of honeyed yams and dirty rice
       caring—fragile and constant
       connections
       how to write a story
       how to live our story
       how to make our lives:
one dazzling orb

The Carroll Poems

A Poem About Hooking Up

I hooked you
in my ear
to phone you
right
at that precise moment
when you woke up
to hear the call

I'm wearing this earring
like determination

The image is
linked loops and green sunlight
two cheeks resting
on the same
certain love

Waking With the Princess

*(at Hampshire)**

Curtainless
through the window
to the bright slopes
of her lying

breast mounds, folded arms
long
          on peace

Preferring sleep
to too much love

Eyes opening on sky, high truth
Voice laying it—clearly—
          in my ear
as we wake
in amber

---

*From certain locations on the grounds of Hampshire College, Massachusetts, one can see a range of hills which resembles a recumbent woman. Legend has it that she is an Indian princess who committed suicide when deserted by her lover.

Kissing deep
        into her mouth
her early morning taste
rising
like orange sun
over coffee brown hills

light

heavy, with cream

then
        stirring

▼

I Want You

I want you on this level
sitting here with me
feeling the breeze
watching the trees
blow
sun up, day starting
you and me asking
the time-worn question,
"How did you sleep last night?"
drinking coffee and
swapping our crazy dreams

I know I'm mixing modes,
confusing levels
like when I said
"I'm crazy being without you"
or wrote, wryly,
about plummeting
into despair

I know the plane we touch on
is spaceless and timeless
has progressed to the fifth dimension
and beyond

There
we're always holding hands
        and kissing
you drizzling your strange love
        in my open mouth
me disappearing constantly
underneath your belly
and finding myself
on the lockscrew
        of our eyes

I know that's somewhere else
and this isn't heaven,
but the bleedthrough, sweet baby,
        is killing me

edges jumping out of place
and seams unraveling
stupid borders that don't hold
and the silences keep
filling up with you

who sits on the rim of my longing
sheering through walls
like some sky-drawn oracle
and still
you can't come to me

on this level
where I know all this
(I know, I know)
is incorrect

Muse

My muse does not come to me
on wings of white
resplendent in Doric charms,
draped cleanly about a classic pond
No, she is not full
        of Attic ease

Her appearances are quite unlike
Milton's heavenly visitations—
although they too come nightly
and always
from above

She does not settle upon my pen
to give me counsel
or lure me, sylphlike,
to the devil's den

I can't depend on her—

At all

She's a nutmeg golden woman
who sits in the cafe sun—
drinking beer,
maybe thinking about her own sad story
(which she is not inspired to write)

Woo her with coke, with smoke,
with booze
angling her flight
and loosening her halting tongue

The rhythms laid-back Black
that pipe her
sometimes to me
sometimes to airier poets
          promising Lotus

(Which line is not pentameter)

Though the discipline is just as hard—
to wait for her
watching
when the dew is wet
and a soft ring in the night
could be
my call to grace

Loving (In Place)

It was a place where sisters played
a plain, a plateau of grassy wind
and dry gold
Nothing moved.
There was a silence there that I had
              never heard before
which frightened me momentarily,
made me wonder if all the music had died down and gone

And we kept touching
the feel of girlish sisters
learning self through same and other self
sexless as sand
but as sensual as the need to sleep
or cry

All our loving works—and we came home
laughing—from the playground and
the carnival rides, hugging,
happy at all the fun we'd shared—
tumbling in the secret rolling through our smiles

Then it was a pool of peace—
again, a still silence, where we clung
surrounded by nothing but our own two selves
The waters drained away—
as we came up, looked clearly at each other,
and saw that it was good.
Creation happens all the time,
and strong love is a healer.

There are no metaphors, no stories
for where I'm spacing now—
you fallen from the shelf above behind me—
me turning as desolate as the park bench
            where we wept

Sun dries, sun lies
then runs behind the clouds where, running,
I can't get to—no matter how I try

I see warm rooms, quiet chaos
your grandmother's marvelous lace
hanging a shrouded blessing above our heads
There are books, and music—
no curtains, but lots of windows
high light and ocean's breathing moving in

Fine things living daily—
like good china at breakfast and beauty breaking
on the edge of dirt
(like you)
Demesnes for your silent spirit,
neat places to put my order in

Although there is no floor plan handy—
and workable agendas for even our speaking
have not been formalized

Fasting

I refuse to write another sadass poem

Thousands die daily of famine in East Africa
and my liberal acquaintances think Anderson
      is a saviour

Why, then, should I phrase a poem
      of personal bloat and void
when, for weeks past now, I've known with you
a joy so fierce
it blazed my body with Kirlian light
etching peace which heaven could envy

One disappointment is not enough to mourn:
      Rosa Ingram spent twelve long years in prison
      for saving her farm against a Georgia white man
and Assata, sister, is still not free
Children in Haiti are choking on garbage,
      while a coal-dark Bahamian brother
      retches up paper scraps

Didn't swimming in the sunset ocean
      with the tide taking grief away
teach me anything?—about come and go, ebb and flow,
      flow and loss, the changing constant,
      and faith—like love—which stays the same

But I have trouble coping with starvation
Though poor and Black in capitalist America,
I grew up with my belly full
(my father overworked his heart to do it)—
and even now I can't not eat
      more than one day at a time

A Ugandan mother hands her bowl of corn meal
   to three skeletal babies
as old men and women fall, making plump hyenas happy

You fill me up
like breadfruit, yam, sweet melon, and coconut milk
This early morning hunger is just a little thing
Though it's killing me, I won't die—

Our love is like a burning candle
eating air
in the midday sun

Totem and tattoo

You are the print
      I can't erase
the yardstick—broken—
      I measure
        each new love by

V

Jamaica
Journal

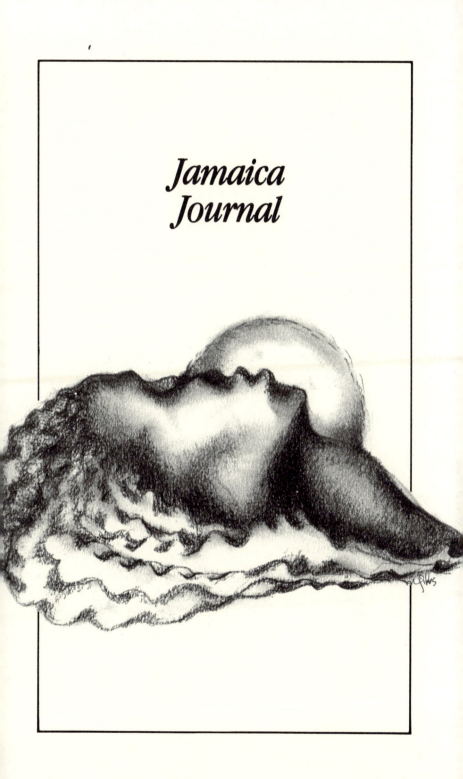

The Bear

"...reflection intruding between my eyes and vision. Not to see myself but to see."

Margaret Atwood, Surfacing

Looking like a bear lumbering
    or the shape of the sun, red-orange-yellow
        spots shimmering like fire
    my own face—even
        blocking the way

If I could see past the lake into the mountains,
    the forest past the trees,
        my own reality trapped in a maze of lies

Things would be easy
    then

I could fly past reason, reasons, and the glare
    of artificial light
into the shining path of water—
        heartbeat skipping and the sound of falling herb,
        brown life growing at my back

I could come to you in season—
    full with blood

Now I give up my own two eyes:
    The sea does not stumble
    and Jah's stars fall with purpose.

Love Words: Spoken

Those are little things, he said

The big thing
is to have this man
whose morning praises
pull me up from sleep
kept dream-sweet by his love
Who made me know
the power of mountains
and why God created stars
and whose laving me in the ocean
was the baptism I needed
to cleanse my timid spirit
Whose voice is the sound of reason
whose palm on my back steadies me
His feet walk straight earth paths
beside me
Shunning concrete like ways of evil
His face—though darkly scoured
by years hard living—
warms me clear as the dawning sun

The important thing
is that he fits my body
perfect as cut cloth
when we tingle like current together
That my soul rests—comfortable—in his
drawing sustenance from the same deep source
and spiraling upward
to new worlds of sight and beauty

It's a big thing
that my heart opens wide
for all dark children
and my vibration
pulls smiles from strangers
that my hands give freely
of the goods I have to share
and family is now more than a word
My limbs are rooting firm
my blood running red
in African strength and struggle

I honor this cherishing man
who makes me laugh
helps to make me whole
who tells me I'm alright
and then I am
Whose gifts turn separation
into a bearable illusion
whose precious self shatters
my world
with joy

At My Age

At my age
now
I can see beauty
in the deep black shadows
of these green hills

Can appreciate the stealthy mold
fuzzing up the shoes in my closet
after fourteen days of rain

Dusk now is just as lovely as the sunset
Broad daylight as enchanting as the moon

Baby lizards play like children
        about my feet
and the drab little hummingbird in this red ixora
        surprises secret joy

At my age
now
I have taken up dancing
        and lip gloss
gone in for fashion
        and frivolity
vamp my hair into flying sexiness

I will speak my mind to whoever dares to listen:
　　　teach my son about heaven and the spirits
　　　warn daughters about the sweet and sour
　　　　　　heaviness of men
　　　crack jokes with the corner idlers when I pass
　　　tell brown and black people about Blackness
　　　　　　babies about their brothers in South Africa
　　　hold hands and run, shout clearly with my sisters
　　　preach sun and flow to every frozen soul
　　　　　　who chills my path

I will leap up! speak up!
without fear of ridicule or broken bones

Crazy, you see, is the freest country
　　　in the world

Don't tell me—in other words—
about your fears of growth and change

Don't tell me what I should have done at fifteen
what was made to look good on flighty twenty-two-year-olds
how big, respectable women are supposed to act
what I should say, what I should do
then, what will people think? think, what will people say?

Look
I can't be bothered with such foolishness
now
at my age

Zora in Accompong *

In Accompong
Zora entered another world

Black magic stilled the hills
and made her listening ears
ring red with wonder

When she left
she spit her spirit in the wind
and disappeared between a crack of sunlight
through the hazy, sacred green

* During her April to September 1936 stay in Jamaica, Zora Neale
Hurston, Afro-American writer and folklorist, lived with the
Maroons in Accompong, where their medicine man hushed a
mountain of singing frogs to demonstrate his power.

Bluestime: Allusions

Since I'm sitting here crying
these tears must be about something

The need to find myself
on the near side
of a faraway mountain,
to lie curled up like a baby
in a strong pair of pitying arms

Did Sojourner Truth's breasts swell,
womb bleed, and eyes run red
with water?
What did Harriet and Nanny know
about periodic female pain?

No woman, Bob said
No cry

But where
in this brazen landscape
are the three little birds
to sing sweet songs
for me?

▼

Dear Pastor

(after the Kingston, Jamaica daily Star, "the people paper")*

(Hum/Sing): God gave Moses a rainbow sign
             No more water, but the fire next time

Dear Pastor:

I am a fifteen-year-old schoolgirl. I was always taught that sex before marriage is a sin. But my boyfriend tells me that if two people love each other, it's alright. Should I give in and listen to him or what? It is getting harder and harder for me to tell him no.

Dear Pastor:

Last weekend I went to Negril and met a very nice girl. I spent the night with her and she inveigled me to try a little cocaine. Now, urinating hurts me and I have headaches everyday. What do you think is wrong with me?

Dear Pastor:

I've always wanted to have a child and I have been a good mother to my baby daughter, who is three years old. When she was born, she seemed normal and healthy—only a little slow. She walked at fifteen months, but she still can't say too many words. Should I be worried about her development?

---

*These letters are not direct transcriptions, but imaginary constructions suggested by the "Dear Pastor" column of the *Star.*

78

Dear Pastor:

Even though my husband and I have always had a happy sex life, he no longer seems to be interested in me that way. He goes out constantly with his two best friends from work and even stays at one of their houses overnight. Do you think that he is becoming a homosexual, or could he have been like that all the time and I just didn't recognize the signs? Please advise me, as I have no one else to ask and I would like to try and save my marriage if I can.

Dear Pastor:

I am a domestic helper with four children. I am still young and do not look too bad. But I keep out of trouble on the job. My man though is still jealous. He accuses me of other men and beats me when he has had too much rum to drink. What must I do?

People live daily, hard lives under fire—
    nuclear power melting down, freedom boiling in South
        Africa
    gunmen blazing right next door, M-16's in the shopping
        center
    burning homes and feverish babies
    cane and ganja fields aflame
    bombs exploding throughout the world—
But what really scorches them
is the heat in their own beds and kitchens
the heart-searing hotness trapped beneath their own zinc roofs

Dear Pastor:

I have a lot of problems. You see, they worry me, they worry me until I think I'm going off my head. My best friend tells me that I should come out of the house and do something. Do you agree with her?

Dear Pastor:

My grandfather told me that the world had already been destroyed by flood and the next time it would be fire. I've been looking at all the tidal waves and earthquakes—plus the weeks and weeks of rain we've been having lately—and wondering if the world could be destroyed again by water. What do you think?

(Hum/Sing, slowing): God gave Moses a rainbow sign
No more water but the fire next time
No more water but the fire next time
No more water but the fire next time...

V

Short Poem

à la Langston Hughes

What I've learned in Jamaica
is how much you can live without

How little water you need to bathe
What to do when the lights go out

Where to go when there's no gas
How leaders remain silent
        while the people shout

Sister to pain, and not unacquainted with grief

This poem
> knows no restraint
It cries out
> Lord, Lord help me
> in the night

This poem knows
> that strength fails
> just as much as weakness—
but that tenderness, too,
> can be another trap

Everything that's broken
> can not be mended—
In hard times
> you're the doctor
> and the patient too

This poem knows
> that silence holds no answers
knows spoken truth
> is not always understood
that every body
> is not made for struggle
every spirit
> can not be tamed to love...

This poem breaks down in the middle
in bitter anguish
Oh, Lord, Lord,
Lord, Lord help me
through the night

V

Soothing An Unquiet Spirit

(from the Tangerine Flat, St. Mary)

Sit in the sun—
       with a little protection
Follow the arc
       of a high-flying bird
Watch a mongoose skitter, a lizard change colors,
       orange throat flashing from, first, black skin
          then green

Think—
       quietly
Breathe—
       deeply
Here comes shadow
There go clouds

Stay still as banana leaves
       when no breeze is blowing
Listen carefully to the trees
       as they begin to talk,
Their counsel suspended
       in a gentle patois

Don't think—
Don't think—
Just feel

Then play with the butterflies
Applaud the red ginger

Get up—
      smiling
And continue to live

"And life. . . .": A Story

In the middle of her domestic crisis
she woke up hungry—
found a banana and made herself
a cup of tea

The baby cried next door
The St. Andrew Cesspool Emptiers
      rumbled up and serviced pits
      across the street,
      while the neighborhood PNP organizer
      began his Sunday rounds

She noticed that the sun was shining yellow brightly
      but that the air itself
      was very, very still

Her son came out of his room
      and scrambled eggs for breakfast
They talked about parties
      and water as an antidote
      for drinking too much alcohol

Her husband returned
      from buying the morning paper
He set his shoes outside the kitchen door
      to catch some air

She worked, took a nap, ate a No. 11 mango
      watched the overtime excitement
      of the World Cup football match

Her period stopped

She and her husband had another foolish argument
        (which was really about ego needs and the use of power)
After tying on his sneakers
        he walked out the front door
        of her life
She finished marking
        her last two examination papers

V

A Jazz Poem

*for Michele**

Lie low—
     and love

This is the season
     for silence
     and deep feeling
     no questions or threats
     promises or open compromises
     togetherness built on
     nothing but need
     quick, sharp
     blood knowing how to seek
     its own salvation

But such abstractions scatter
     this muted moonlight
     clichéd beauty of a lone
          coconut tree
     giving shape to the silver sky:
     the only definition one can trust—
     a fact
     as true as hummingbird flight
     the arch of a lithe brown body
     clotted pain whimpering in boxes—
          (Nobody knows
          what it's all about)

---

*To be read/heard to the music of Archie Shepp and Dollar Brand.

This old world is not civilized
Grace plays no violins
Drums beat
         some other rhythm
Maniac cowboys
         riding herd
         over rock/dark people
         refusing the staged stampede
         resisting the old orders

As usual
this poem wants to hide its hand
its origins
in your shoulder,
your clear-eyed images
         of heart and struggle

As usual
I want to hush my mouth
and become a universal voice
chanting down Babylon
         in broad accents of the people

But what I really want is for
this thumping in my chest
to break clean through

I want to become myself

I want the stolen spirits
       to gather at night
       and teach me
       another language

But I'm afraid
if I start talking,
I may not stop
for another hundred years

V

Ongiving

Some people weigh and balance
and count the cost
Make change to the last worthless penny
Hug tight the shrinking dollar as it slides

But what price brotherhood or sistren?
Which sales tag do we pin on love?

What I pass on to you
is bounty from the universe:

Lunch money a teacher gave me in third grade
The term dress to say my speeches in
Bad colds and cancer which did not catch me
Yellow and white light protecting me and kin
All the fellowships, friendships, prayers,
good wishes,
good vibes, luck
which keep me alive and standing

returning, turning to its source

Give thanks—and give back

Living in the spirit is one spiral dance

From each according to her riches
To each according to his need,
Met on every rung
and climbing higher, higher

Give thanks—and give back

The widow's mite, a golden smile
Fifty cents to a hungry child
Strength sometimes when you don't quite have it
One more step at the end of a mile

And give thanks, give thanks

Generosity, like mercy, is not strained—
Give back

Though dollars fall, godpeople still rising
Love expands
Some folks do care

Give thanks

Give thanks

When Storm Clouds Gather

"Jah wouldn't be so wicked,"
the Rasta brother in Junction said,
waiting at the deserted bus stop
splotchy
one cricket Sunday afternoon

Would never leave us stranded
        while the rains come down
Would never turn our nightmare fantasies
        into truth

Red ink or black coffee
        will not spill on the manuscript
The house will not burn
        with the symbols of self inside

When the mother dies
        another rock
        will soon be ready
When beauty goes
        wisdom will descend
        to take her place

The lock will not break
the auric ring has no give
You'll never turn and find
that bogey man
laughing
at the bathroom door
The sidewalk between the car's slam
and sweet enclosure
will always remain in the moonlight
street light unmolested

You will not die before your time
in the always far-off future
when blessings—like honor and grandchildren—
are nimbused around your still-bright head

Yemaya's waves will not turn treacherous
The plane will not drop
between houses
or gray waters
or the dense jungle trees
        of some unknown African forest

Jah would not be so wicked

Malevolence must not fall
        like rottening coconuts
        upon thy naked head
The dread menace of the universe
        must keep its frozen distance

Faith—a charm—
Arms and comfort
Hold

▼

Welcome Home

The only people Miss U.S.A.
wants to enter her free country
are blonde-haired, sunburnt tourists
with one piece of luggage
some straw
and a duty-clear bottle of rum

For the rest of us—
permanently colored by tropic suns
and southern cane fields,
it's one long line of interrogation
our progress stopped by red lights,
by beefy agricultural inspectors
          with pestilent tongues, and
customs officials whose straight-haired darkness
               declares that their ancestors, too,
               came off some other boats

There is nothing to do but wait—
beside carton boxes filled with
our bammy and belongings,
trying not to think about
the illegal half-dozen mangoes
or the life all set to ambush us
beyond the swinging doors

We shift in the weight
of fake gold medallions
tight suits left over from splendid weddings
tie up red hair ribbons,
other loose ends

We move through—
inch, by foot, by inch
We look evil, or smile
answer the questions, take the knife,
say "thank you" for the government tape
which straps us back together

Welcome!
Welcome Home!

▼

Of peace, I say *

On these hot afternoons
I seek the moist coolness
of your downstairs bed
and imagine that I am Winnie—
stepping with regal lightness
through bars of iron make-believe—
inviting Nelson to lie, long sweetheart
cherished comrade
rest for a just-us moment,
on the warm red, black and green
of this freedom spread I dream for you

The embankment is always clover fresh
and full of promise
the southeast breeze a sea song
salt with hope
A place of lull between battles
in what must seem to all of us
a never-ending war

You'd pick the wildflowers
if you had space to put them
but, lover, here—pretty—sweetheart
tie this bright bunch inside your head—
to the spot where the future opens
like an all-seeing eye
to the mole, the crease, the scar
the locks lengthening with knots and care

---

*With thanks to Lorna Goodison and her "Bedspread" poem.

Dark sunny rooms are alive with tiers of words
and unspent kisses tremulously touch—
We hear the hum of a perfect earth
move together in time to that sacred music
giving thanks for these clear afternoons
which turn flesh into atoms and air

Of peace, I say,
peace, my brother,
and universal love

V

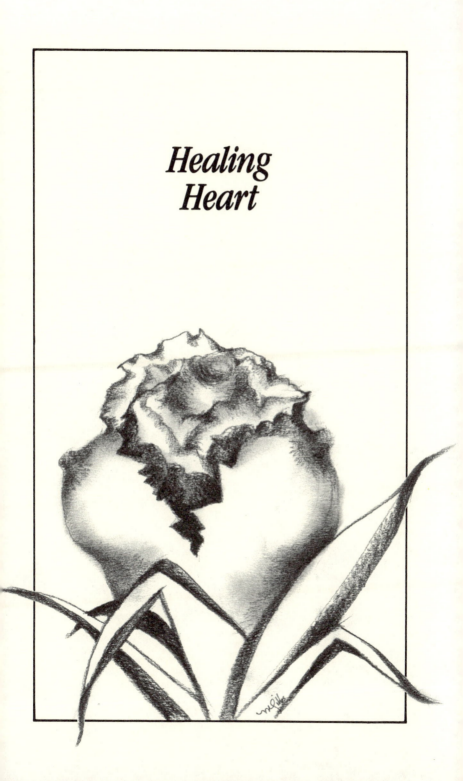

Healing Heart

Invocation

I do not need the contorted fury
of any more angry men—
whether they wear
the face of God
or of
my second husband

Little girl, inside me
Love
smiles on you

All the fathers failed you
The one who made you
and then ran off
to new adventures
That other one—the good man—
who gave you food
but could not
call you daughter

Come, little woman
inside me
Find in my arms
your proper blessing
and this healing love

Young Girls' Blues

"It's not so good
to be born a girl"
                    ntozake shange

i.

Who could ever hurt
a pretty little sweetheart
like you?

ii.

Shake those nasty hips
on down to the ground
You see, wom-ney
you see

iii.

Sitting on laps and knees

Snakes in my bed—nightmare
long black snakes
hanging pendulous from the ceiling

Commotion to the other side
of the house
Back to bed—
snakes and fear

The drunk brothers, uncles, family friends you had to put up with–to treat like they made sense even as they acted like they didn't–to respect when they didn't respect themselves and disrespected you; to serve drinks and supposedly sobering food– and then to pick up quarters and dollar bills (too young for Billie Holiday's pinching thighs on the table, but knowing somehow that you'd been bought anyway, were selling more than the trip to the kitchen or the corner store).

The rough, bearded embraces, held too tight and too long. Why was everybody laughing–except you? Slipping out and away from the reek and the heaviness, stains which have never, never, never been wiped clean.

v. Breastplates

Tender breast buds
brushed with a cankerous pleasure
pinched with too-palpable pain

What did the two men say
to one another
when you told your mother
about the 50¢ touch?

Perversion of springing pleasure
of body-based joy
hanging it up
with guilt and danger

Encoding the tingling breasts
and tightening thighs
which swell forever
with pornographic images
of the cheapened self

No! A silent stop—
wrestling down the elastic
of the little white bolero blouse

Making love in college
with the shame
and clean brassieres
in place

No! Taking off everything
but the lightly-padded 32-A

Never believing
any lover's hands
were small enough
to be satisfied
with just that much chest
to hold

vi.

The body remembers
what the mind forgets

Repression is
the habit of forgetting

Remembering:
like chasing a dream down
by the tail

vii.

Every night
for the past nine days
dreaming
Varnette Honeywood images

viii.

The past:
a smell like stale urine
and ashes
burning

ix.

Pink-Pink—
Mrs. Mary Pink Favors—
married to Mr. Henry
better known as Buck

One day, she said
the blood will come
streaming down your legs—
then you better be careful
what you do with the boys

No wonder
those first brown spots
didn't tell me a thing

x.

Jackie's mother
Celeste
"Mammy Cat"
to the women
who disliked her—
for reasons
I'll never know

xi.

Tiny
(Earl her brother)
in the tenement dungle
of Abbie Street's seventeen hundred block:

"And Tiny wants water
Hold 'em, Joe"
"And Tiny wants water
Hold 'em, Joe"

To miracle straighten
her small humped back
put flesh on the bones
her mother couldn't,
dark, dark woman
with nicotine eyes—
and no answers

I think they buried her,
Tiny,
in a pretty white dress
her nice hair curled
in shiny black water waves—

xii.

Childhood
is a landscape
filled with monsters

xiii.

I got the blue
She got the pink
She got the red
I got the blue

My color
made the difference

We both got the hair ribbons
yards and yards
of satin and peau-de-soie
The veined grosgrain fabric
wide enough for a sunbonnet
fluted and tied
into monstrous and fanciful bows
dwarfing my nappy-headed pigtails
my knots crying out
for some other way
to be beautiful—and black

I didn't feel pretty
like a long-braided girl,
like Shirley Temple neither
even with her imitation sausages
hanging from my ears

Every Sunday
on the way to church
I threw those ribbons
in the Norma Street ditch
told my mother
"I lost it"
"It musta fell off"
"I don't know how come
          it's not on my head"—

Every Sunday
she sent me out pretty
and dying—
from beribboned shame
and my own plain ugliness

xiv. The Preacher: Ruminations

Scene 1

The motel in Minden
(always long, car rides)
becoming winter
(fall or spring)—
his classic longjohns
tight and surprising
under the tailored suit
cut to fit his long, skinny body—
long, skinny joint
washed afterward
in the naked, spotty bowl
a cut above the Taylor Street Courts
notches below what he afforded later
after his fame and membership grew

Scene 2

The football game—Cowboys losing
"On their period" that particular day, we joked
Whiskey in a sack with motel ice and coke

I came third.

The real thing

She was the nice girl
reticent and neat—
kept her voice—and her dress
both down
Deferent
made him a sandwich
as he watched
his image in the world
unfolding
the trim little figure
swell
with future sons—
the Missus at home
who always—late at night—
could turn, he said,
his body hot

So, what was it
that I did?—
listening to my own devaluation,
smart girl playing whore
without even getting paid—
cheaper than the two dollar screwdrivers,
the price of one.

Power

Religious power—passion
Love of God and the erotic

He told me about
hard-on's in the pulpit
about prayers to the Father
to take his sin away:

Me running off
like dirty soapsuds
down salvation's drain

Coda: Men Washing

Right after sex
the hygienic ritual:

Legs spread before the wash bowl
heads bent in concentration
on the thing
which must be cleaned—
soaping the shaft, the head
turning back the skin
rinsing away
whatever might be catching
getting rid of dirt and slime

Women
hold it all
themselves
inside

V

The Rice and Peas Farewell

I'm not gonna be
your rice and peas
no more

Food
on your plate

Spread for the taking

Eye appeal
Just-right, ample portion
Designed with only you
in mind

Full filling dish

Eat it up
'Nyam it down

Eat it up
'Nyam it down

On the side
with Sunday dinner

Warm it up next morning
Fry the plantain for lunch
Why not have a taste
for the midnight snack

Just eat it up
'Nyam it down

Now it's all gone, baby
All gone

The Way It Is (Right Now)

Ah, I see:

Before I can make it to the top
I have to get taken down
all the way
to the raw wood splintered floor,
scratch
jugking my heart
and scraping my rusty knees

And I'm sick of smelling turpentine
(the shit I had to use myself
to scrub my own way down here)
Do I have to mop this motherfucker
with my tears?
lick the sawdust with my tongue?

I need to be using that for kissing.
The next one who tastes
what I've been holding
is going to get their head blown off!
It's that deep
that sweet and real,
a straight shot all the way
to so much knowing love
so much to give
that...

I can't even talk about it.

▼

Counting Cost

i.

Walk out the door

Too much pain
too much limitation—
Leave that woman-thing
      that mother-bind
behind

ii.

Images:

I.
Fifteen months old—
Us returning from the interview trip
      to Midlands, Michigan
      to Elizabeth, New Jersey
      to Chicago, Illinois

One:
the red bib coveralls
the red piano
unplayed
no smile of greeting
no outstretched arms—
taking what was given
as early as that point
reaching out for nothing
which was not there

Times two:
The swollen face
blueblack from eye to chin—
The babysitter said he fell,
her spare white face
nipped and frosty language
offering no details and less apology

His face
the same passivity
uncried questions
            in the old man eyes

The rational approach to childrearing requires:
no angry accusations, no alarm
no swooping arms of pity
no tears, never
no tears

Without really looking at one another
we collect the child and go on home

II.
Fifteen years old—
In the house of empty rooms
full of nothing but furniture
and fancy shades pulled down
against the evening sun,
dustbeams caught in yellow light
the only signs of life

My timid rescues are slight
            and temporary
Aloneness is the dependable order of the day

Cheery goodbyes
which did not fool the silence—
By then the old unasked, unanswered question
not even a feeble echo in the void:
"Mommy, can I come
      and live with you?"

iii.

Walk out the door—

Away from meals
of fried pork chops and frozen string beans,
of the feminine mystique turned black—and blue
Needing a larger self
a whole, new way of being
in that tragic drama
where all the characters
play the parts of ghosts
and end up dying
as the world turns,
as the curtains fall

Cry all the unshed tears many long years later
Look the damned and bloody monsters
      in their midnight face
Count the cost
Feel the pain

Cry it all out—
Unblock the aching head
    the clouded eyes
    the choked-up throat
    the banded heart
    the knotted entrails
    the swollen womb
    the two tied tubes

    the way to health
    to self—
    forgiveness
    love
    and joy

V

Ron II

Dead would be more romantic

Then I could hear
from the lips
of your grieving mother
how you spent
the last ten years,
get cameo shots of you
with Scott and his baby brother,
learn where you set your foot
and spread your laughter,
how it was
your hands and voice
fell still

But I would rather find you live
and living in San Francisco
the scar and the frown
the grin and tears intact,
your pleasant face still strong
you cracking jokes
about the thinning hair
which signed for you
your Donne-man fate

I would rather feel all over
your bleeding kindness,
learn once again
if a white boy's touch
can heal

▼

Somebody, Some Body

I need somebody
to touch me
in a healing way

Somebody

Some body

to touch me—
with love

somebody
who can hold
this depth of pain

hold me
crying tears
for every woman
whose
being a woman
has ever
made her cry

Unshed grief
running out slowly
in a river
of cleansing salt

▼

Being Clear About It

Being
in pain

It's not like
your head hurts
or you have a backache
or your arthritis
has been acting up
that day

Being
in pain

is like
the middle of another country
        an empty sea of water
a twilight moonscape
     in the high Sierras

some nowhere place
between the landing
and the
letting go

V

Another Rhythm

Little girl
grown up

Little grown-up girl

We've cried
We've held ourselves
We've rocked
to the rhythm
of tears
turning pain
to peace

Rise up now
woman
Adorn yourself

Let your light
and beauty
shine

You, Too

And do I weep for you, too
my little reddish-brown sweetheart?

Defying kên, not keeping still
I locked my body tight against you,
        shut you out

Then met the one
whose piercing magic opened me,
but could not coax you
from your hiding place

Now here you stand
my sweet reddish-brown baby,
little girl I never had
I love you

Who told you...?

(for Edie)

Who said
you could keep notebooks—
like Virginia Woolf?

Like Lessing's heroine
four in different colors
      one for dreams
      one for poetry
      one a journal
      the last to hold work ideas
         in their place

Who gave you time
to record your thoughts?
Who told you that your thoughts
were worth recording?

"Nobody—
but myself"

Pants For True

We had spent the day together

That evening
I had on my colorful, sophisticated
            African drummer pants
a soft black belt
pulling in my waist
giving the difference with my hips
a deadly edge

Talk, communication continued
He told me,
"You're what I've been waiting for"
we looking the questions
into each other's eyes

"Touch me," I said

It wasn't true.

▼

About Grandmothers and Mothers

My mother had a grandmother
I didn't

She had Aunt Winnie
Black Creek, cooking woman
church-founding, proud-strong woman
married to Anthony Sims

They migrated from some homeland in Alabama
to the oil plots and spreading gardens
of East Texas

Aunt Winnie died
when my mother was fifteen
She only had her mother then,
a Noma who sometimes worked away from home
and orphaned her through death
two scant years later

My mother had a grandmother
and a mother
and neither one of them lasted her
into womanhood—

Girls without mothers
mother themselves,
sometimes become mothers
much too soon

She—at seventeen—
a wild thing running,
the baby dropping
from her slender arms

V

Legacy/Repeat After Me

My great-grandmother
compacted all her grief
until it festered as a life sore
in her side
She huddled it close
changed her pus-stained rags
in secret
Nobody in the family
knew about her shame
until they smelled the cancer
which ate her breath away

My grandmother
never found her proper nourishment
They said she ate "too much cornmeal"
Pellagra, we call it today—
a deficiency disease
which killed my grandmother
little, quick woman
who never stopped moving
until she died

My mother lives out
their lives of lack and limitation
old pains, old wounds, old angers,
resentment, grief, fear, and shame
Her milk soured in the mouth
of my baby brother
Thirty-eight years later
they cut the whole breast off
Lack of self-love, love—criticism
hardening her joints
she still holds on
holds on

All this they willed to me
this freighted legacy
I want
to cast away

I say—to myself—
repeat after me:

Throw out those old clothes
        (Let the latest and hottest fashions
        take their place)

Give the leftover spoonsful to the dog
        (God will set a fresh dish
        on the table)

Do not hoard pieces of string, clean rags,
or colored ribbons
        (Say: What I need will be at hand
        when I need it)

Give up extreme gratefulness for pennies
        (so that thanks for thousands
        can be made)

Give away love
        (then love, and then more love
        will fill the place)

Let go fear
        (Come power
        and possibility)

Expel anger
     (Welcome joy)

Let go of children
     (who will then embrace you happily
     at every turn)

Release pain and dis-ease
     (Spirit pushes
     the healing through)

And now
I say:
repeat after me

Good Question

Perhaps I never wanted
to be born
into that family

They tried to sweeten
my infant spirit,
fed me sugar
and still more sugar

All it did
was poison me

I erupted in helpless fury
my anger swelling up in boils
on my back
in my head,
the wisdom I brought with me
saying (nobody listened) that
love should be healthy
clean and pure

So the doctors chided
and my mother cried
They shaved my head
They lanced the boils

Who then smiled
at the tiny, bald-headed girl?
Gave pretty looks
to the little dark
little female child
whose cuteness
was buried in plaster?

Seeing the fading evidence
the old scars barely visible
on my grownup back,
attentive girlfriends sometimes ask,
incredulous:
"Who stabbed you?"

Dumping Harry Claggett

Yes
the bastard took advantage of me
Climbed his old ass up top my sweet young pussy
and enjoyed himself
And he didn't give me the new dress he had promised,
after showing me all his credit cards

I know
somebody should have taught me better
should have made me see
there were other, nicer ways to be a woman
should have hipped me
should have pulled my coat
to the fact that the real pearl of greatness
the inside gem of self
truly does have no price

So this low-lifed motherfucker
is still humping away inside me
swelling my belly with fibroid tumors
raising up headaches behind my opening eyes—
the nastiest piece of shit
I want to dump today.
Like these four squat heavy ugly glasses,
he has no more business
sitting on my precious shelf—
needs to be smashed into loathsome nothing,
stomped into little pieces bit by bit

He shouldn't have taken advantage of me.
He shouldn't have done that to my tender bud—
      blooming blood, rage, anger
      so much pain and tears
So much for these tears, this running nose
as I drive through congestion to the city dump

There is no place in the civilized world
for an angry woman to vent her madness—
to rage like the howling moon
scream like a banshee
break glasses, storm and shout

The drive to the recyclable lot is for employees only.
The guard at the gatehouse of the dump
keeps all non-residents out
(and I don't have my lease on me
to show where I belong).
There is no concrete plot, no idle dumpster
no vacant parking lot
where I can kill this grief

Detoured to the nature preserve,
I bark at the foraging squirrels
yell back at the flying gulls
resist the mock seductions of peace, sea breeze, and sunshine.
think to myself:
This motherfucker does not deserve recycling—
His atoms should not be one with the universe,
nor should his ass feed grass

I pray for all these lunchtime snackers and snoozers
to leave this part of the shore
so I can throw my ugly glasses on the concrete blocks.
Finally, the cars near the back half drive away—
and the sound of the first glass breaking is sweet—
but I can't send up my ceremonial shouts and curses
as I dance around his broken bones.
Shit!

The dump is now even more crowded.
The guard is still on duty.
I swing down an illegal back road,
leave the rest of my garbage
next to a warning sign,
between a running stream with three skinny ground squirrels
and the noxious odors of the waste site
on the other side.

136

Crossing

At the foot of the cross
kneeling before the altar of myself
exorcising demons
with the power of soundings
and universal, mystic law

Showers of blessing
rain from my eyes
My great-grandmother brings comfort
her hand an affirmation on my shoulder

A cry for riddance, for release
becomes its own answer:
Yes, I forgive
and I love everybody—
hugging the old devils
one by one

When Trees Talk

For Patti, Tuck, and Louise

When trees talk
and shrubs dance up to my eyes
in three-dimension
Sun and blue sky kiss
and the butterflies jig
on laughing air

Then I know love
I taste joy
and it does take my breath away—
rolling it back to me
in an ocean of life—
where I can float like jewelled light
for as long
as I shall choose to live

Meeting the Self

She was my sister
black like me
We were lying—
side by side—
sharing rumors and feelings,
testing the energy—
ready to go the magic distance
on its warm and wonderful flow

I looked up at her hair
entangling my eyes
in a thicket of green
leafy branches, luxuriant clover and fern

As I start to tell her
it may now be time
for her to clip, to cultivate it,
I decide to change the message
to say I love her
from my speaking red root
and greenness of heart
to grow, sister, grow

▼

8-5-88

The sound may not be Muddy Waters
or the soul-stirring strains
        of Sister Rosetta Tharpe
or even Mr. Ray Charles, genius
rocking down the generations

Perhaps I didn't step out back in the garden
to pick these mustards myself
although the stems and leaves
on my right hand
are stacking up just the same

This old house skirt
these corn-soft shoes I'm wearing
would be at home
in anybody's yard or kitchen—
as the oil and salt
of many solid women
hum through my veins

My place here
has that feel of peace
the pungent smell of love

I know
today—for sure—
I am somebody's mother

These greens I'm cooking
can nourish you

▼

About the Author

Gloria Theresa (Thompson) Hull was born in 1944 in Shreveport, Louisiana to a working poor home which eventually consisted of her mother, father, and a younger brother and sister. She survived Jim Crow racism and the pitfalls of adolescence to graduate from the Booker T. Washington High School and Southern Universtity, then proceeded north for further study at Purdue University, where she earned her Ph.D. degree in 1972. In the six weeks between passing her M.A. examinations and beginning the next school year as a teaching assistant, she gave birth to her only child, Adrian Prentice (whose father was also a doctoral student).

In the early 1970's she launched her career as a university professor and Black feminist literary critic, making outstanding contributions to the newly developing field of Black women's studies. Her publications include four other books, a monograph, and numerous scholarly articles, among which are *All the Women Are White, All the Blacks Are Men, But Some of Us Are Brave: Black Women's Studies* (with P.B. Scott and B. Smith, 1982), *Give Us Each Day: The Diary of Alice Dunbar-Nelson* (1984), and *Color, Sex, and Poetry: Three Women Writers of the Harlem Renaissance* (1987). She has been the recipient of National Endowment for the Humanities, Rockefeller, Ford, and Mellon grants, and spent two fruitful years in Jamaica as a senior Fulbright lecturer (1984-1986). Currently, she is Professor of Women's Studies and Literature at the University of California, Santa Cruz.

Other Titles from Kitchen Table: Women of Color Press

Narratives: Poems in the Tradition of Black Women by Cheryl Clarke, $5.95 paper.

Cuentos: Stories by Latinas, Alma Gómez, Cherríe Moraga, and Mariana Romo-Carmona, eds., $7.95 paper.

Home Girls: A Black Feminist Anthology, Barbara Smith, ed., $12.95 paper.

This Bridge Called My Back: Writings by Radical Women of Color, Cherríe Moraga and Gloria Anzaldúa, eds., $9.95 paper.

A Comrade Is As Precious As a Rice Seedling, Mila D. Aguilar, $6.95 paper.

Seventeen Syllables and Other Stories, Hisaye Yamamoto, $9.95 paper.

Desert Run: Poems and Stories, Mitsuye Yamada, $7.95 paper.

Freedom Organizing Pamphlet Series

#1 *The Combahee River Collective Statement,* Foreword by Barbara Smith, $3.25 paper.

#2 *Apartheid U. S. A.* by Audre Lorde and *Our Common Enemy, Our Common Cause: Freedom Organizing in the Eighties* by Merle Woo, $3.50 paper.

#3 *I Am Your Sister: Black Women Organizing Across Sexualities* by Audre Lorde, $3.50 paper.

#4 *It's a Family Affair: The Real Lives of Black Single Mothers,* by Barbara Omolade, $3.50 paper.

#5 *Violence Against Women and the Ongoing Challenge to Racism,* by Angela Y. Davis, $3.50 paper.

When ordering please include $1.50 for postage and handling for the first book and 50¢ for each additional book. For overseas orders please include $2.00 (U.S.) postage and handling for each book requested. Order from: Kitchen Table: Women of Color Press, P.O. Box 908, Latham, NY 12110.